BOTTLENOSE DOLPHINS

Michael Molnar

LIFE CYCLES
OF MARINE ANIMALS

This edition first published in 2012 in the United States of America by Smart Apple Media.

Smart Apple Media
P.O. Box 3263
Mankato, MN, 56002

First published in 2011 by
MACMILLAN EDUCATION AUSTRALIA PTY LTD
15–19 Claremont St, South Yarra, Australia 3141

Visit our web site at www.macmillan.com.au or go directly to www.macmillanlibrary.com.au

Associated companies and representatives throughout the world.

Copyright text © Michael Molnar 2011

Library of Congress Cataloging-in-Publication Data has been applied for.

Publisher: Carmel Heron
Commissioning Editor: Niki Horin
Managing Editor: Vanessa Lanaway
Editor: Tim Clarke
Proofreader: Paige Amor
Designer: Tanya De Silva
Page layout: Tanya De Silva and Raul Diche
Photo researcher: Sarah Johnson (management: Debbie Gallagher)
Illustrators: Ian Faulkner (**7**, **8**, **10**); Michael Wilkin (**12–25**)
Production Controller: Vanessa Johnson

Manufactured in China by Macmillan Production (Asia) Ltd
Kwun Tong, Kowloon, Hong Kong
Supplier Code: CP January 2011

Acknowledgments

The author and publisher are grateful to the following for permission to reproduce copyright material:

Front cover illustrations by Michael Wilkin.

Back cover photographs: Shutterstock/Marcus Efler (Bottlenose Dolphin underwater), /Four Oaks (Two Bottlenose Dolphins leaping).

Photographs courtesy of: Dreamstime/Gentoomultimedia, 4 (bottom), /Lynne77, **4** (top), Summersea, **29**; Copyright © Brandon Cole. All Rights Reserved, **5**, **26**; Getty Images/Tom Brakefield, **6**, /Stephen Frink, **30**, /Frank Greenaway, **10** (garfish); iStockphoto/IanCale, **11**, /syagci, **28**; Photolibrary/Jeffrey L. Rotman, **7**, **27**, /Splashdown Direct, **9**; Shutterstock/ale1969, **10** (prawn), /criben, **10** (pilchard), /ikopylov, **10** (mullet), /Dmytro Tkachuk, **10** (octopus), /Zloneg, **10** (squid).

While every care has been taken to trace and acknowledge copyright, the publisher tenders their apologies for any accidental infringement where copyright has proved untraceable. They would be pleased to come to a suitable arrangement with the rightful owner in each case.

Contents

Read the story of one bottlenose dolphin's life cycle in these pages.

Words that are printed in **bold** are explained in the Glossary on page 31.

Life Cycles of Marine Animals

Scientists believe that all life on Earth began in the ocean, hundreds of millions of years ago. Today, thousands of different animal **species** live in and around the ocean. No one knows exactly how many different species of **marine** animals there are—hundreds of new species are discovered every year. Although they share the same saltwater **habitat**, all marine animals grow and change differently over time. Each species has its own unique life cycle.

Life Cycles

All living things have a life cycle. An animal's life cycle begins when it is born and is completed when it has young of its own. During their life cycles, different species grow and change in different ways. Everything an animal does throughout its life cycle happens so that it can survive long enough to **reproduce**. Without this circle of life, all living things would become **extinct**.

The life cycles of marine animals can be as different as the animals themselves.

Bottlenose Dolphins

Bottlenose dolphins are one of more than 30 species of dolphin. Each of these species has a different life cycle. Bottlenose dolphins must survive many dangers in order to complete their life cycle.

Dolphins are Mammals

Dolphins look and swim like fish, but they are actually mammals. Mammals are warm-blooded animals that breathe air and care for their young. All female mammals produce milk, which they feed to their young.

Living Together

Bottlenose dolphins are social animals that live together in small groups. These groups are always changing, but are usually made up of between 2 and 15 dolphins. By living in groups and helping each other, dolphins have a better chance of surviving and completing their life cycles.

Bottlenose dolphins swim together in groups, helping and protecting each other throughout their life cycles.

Dolphins are Related to Hippos!

It is believed that dolphins **evolved** from land animals millions of years ago. Today, the closest living relatives of dolphins are hippopotamuses.

What Do Bottlenose Dolphins Look Like?

Over millions of years, bottlenose dolphins have **adapted** to life in the ocean. The shape of their bodies has changed over time to make them great swimmers. They can swim at speeds of more than 21 miles (35 km) per hour.

a sleek, streamlined body to glide through the water

a dorsal fin to help the dolphin balance as it swims fast through the water

thick rubbery skin, with a layer of **blubber** under the surface to keep it warm

pectoral fins to steer and stop

A dolphin's tail has two flukes. By moving its tail up and down, it can push itself through the water.

Female dolphins produce milk to feed their calves. Young dolphins suckle on teats on the underside of their mother's body.

VITAL STATISTICS

Size: more than 9 feet (3 m) long
Weight: up to 800 pounds (400 kg)

Color: gray on their back, fading to almost white on their underside

Large Brains

Dolphins have large brains, which allow them to communicate. They use clicks, whistles, grunts, and squeaks to call to each other. This communication helps dolphins to work together when they hunt in groups.

Length Comparison

Killer whale: 29 feet (9 m)

Bottlenose dolphin: 10 feet (3 m)

Common dolphin: 6.5 feet (2 m)

Spinner dolphin: 6.5 feet (2 m)

Scuba diver: 5.6 feet (1.7 m)

Maui's dolphin: 4 feet (1.3 m)

Instead of nostrils, dolphins have a blowhole on the top of their head. Dolphins breathe through their blowhole when they surface for air.

The dolphin's bottle-shaped nose is called a rostrum. It can be used to dig in the sand and under rocks to find food.

Dolphins have good eyesight and can see in very low light.

Dolphins have between 80 and 100 teeth. They use their teeth to grab and hold their prey. Dolphins cannot chew with their teeth, so they swallow their food whole or tear it into smaller pieces.

Dolphins hear using their lower jaw. Dolphins can hear very well and use sound to communicate and hunt for food.

7

Where Do Bottlenose Dolphins Live?

Bottlenose dolphins live in most oceans and seas around the world. They can be found in many different habitats, such as in sheltered bays close to shore or in deep waters far out to sea.

Bottlenose dolphins live in cooler waters, such as the North Atlantic Ocean around Europe, and warmer waters, such as the South Pacific Ocean around South America.

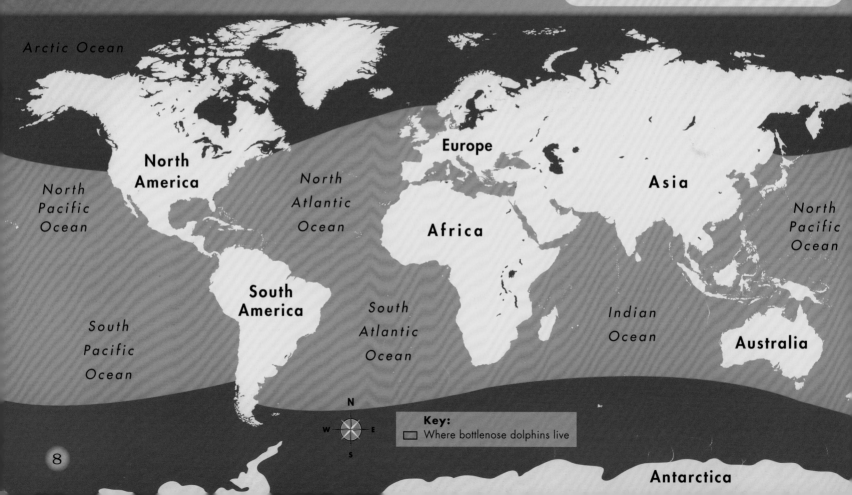

Arctic Ocean

North America

North Pacific Ocean

North Atlantic Ocean

Europe

Asia

Africa

North Pacific Ocean

South America

South Pacific Ocean

South Atlantic Ocean

Indian Ocean

Australia

N
W   E
S

Key:
☐ Where bottlenose dolphins live

Antarctica

Habitats

Bottlenose dolphins have adapted to live in almost all saltwater habitats. Some live in the deep, open ocean, where they travel in large groups, searching for large schools of fish and squid to eat. Other groups of bottlenose dolphins live closer to shore. These smaller groups can often be seen swimming along open beaches, as well as inside harbours, bays and **estuaries**. Bottlenose dolphins prefer water temperatures that are between 50 and 90 degrees Fahrenheit (10 and 32 degrees Celsius).

Home Range

A dolphin's home range is the area in which it lives. Some dolphins have a large home range and can travel long distances in search of warmer water and food. Dolphins living in the cold waters around Scotland, in the United Kingdom, can travel hundreds of miles south during winter. Bottlenose dolphins living in warmer coastal waters often have a smaller home range.

Some bottlenose dolphins live in coastal habitats, such as along open beaches.

What Do Bottlenose Dolphins Eat?

Bottlenose dolphins are **carnivores** that eat many types of marine animals. They are **predators** that have developed many different ways to hunt for food.

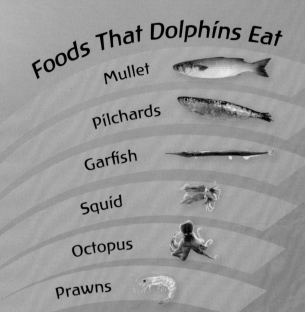

Foods That Dolphins Eat

Mullet

Pilchards

Garfish

Squid

Octopus

Prawns

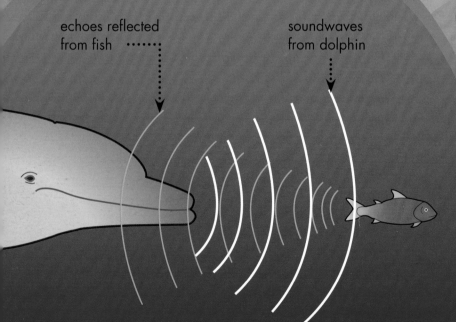

echoes reflected from fish ....>

soundwaves from dolphin

Hunting Using Sound

All dolphins hunt for food using sound. This is called echolocation. They make loud clicking noises and then listen for the echoes to bounce back off objects. Using these echoes, the dolphins can imagine a picture of what is around them. This allows dolphins to find **prey** in dark or dirty water. Bottlenose dolphins can even use echolocation to find fish buried in the sand!

The clicks made by bottlenose dolphins travel as soundwaves through the water. When these soundwaves reach prey such as fish, they bounce back as echoes. These echoes tell bottlenose dolphins where prey can be found.

Hunting in the Open Ocean

Bottlenose dolphins that live in the open ocean usually hunt in larger groups. They travel long distances looking and listening for schools of fish. Once they find the fish, the dolphins work together to surround the school. The dolphins slowly herd the fish toward the surface. Trapped between the surface and the surrounding dolphins, the fish cannot escape. The dolphins then take turns swimming through the school, eating fish as they go.

Deep Diving

Dolphins that live in the open ocean can dive more than 1,600 feet (500 m) deep searching for food.

Hunting Closer to Shore

Bottlenose dolphins living closer to shore work in groups to herd small schools of fish into shallow water. The fish have no room to escape, so the dolphins have no trouble grabbing the trapped fish before swallowing them whole.

Dolphins sometimes chase fish out of the water, grabbing them in midair as they jump to escape.

THE LIFE CYCLE OF A
BOTTLENOSE DOLPHIN

The life cycle of a bottlenose dolphin is similar to those of many other mammals. Female dolphins feed and protect their young calves until they are able to care for themselves. Once fully grown, dolphins can **breed**, have young and complete their life cycle.

1 A Bottlenose Dolphin is Born

Bottlenose dolphins usually give birth to a single calf. After she has given birth, the mother feeds and protects her young. She turns onto her side so the newborn calf can suckle milk from teats on her underside.

4 Mating and Giving Birth

Bottlenose dolphins are ready to **mate** between 5 and 12 years of age. Female dolphins mate with several males, and the female dolphin will become **pregnant**. After 12 months, the female gives birth to a single live calf and her life cycle is complete.

2 Growing Up

As it grows, the young calf spends its day playing close to its mother. Play is very important for young dolphin calves because it teaches them to swim and hunt. The young dolphin starts catching its own food after about six months. It can also continue to suckle for several years.

3 Becoming an Adult

After several years, the young dolphin no longer needs the protection of its mother, but it may stay with her for a long time. Dolphins are very social animals and even adult dolphins prefer to remain living in groups.

In warm water close to the coast,
a bottlenose dolphin calf is born.

Her mother gently guides her to the surface so she can take her first breath.

The young calf can swim from the moment she is born, but she is not yet strong enough to survive on her own. Her mother is very protective and stays by her side.

The young calf is hungry.
She nudges her mother to let her know
she wants some milk.

Her mother slows her swimming
and rolls onto her side, so the young
calf can reach her teats.

The young calf needs to
suckle several times an
hour, so she stays close to
her mother's side.

15

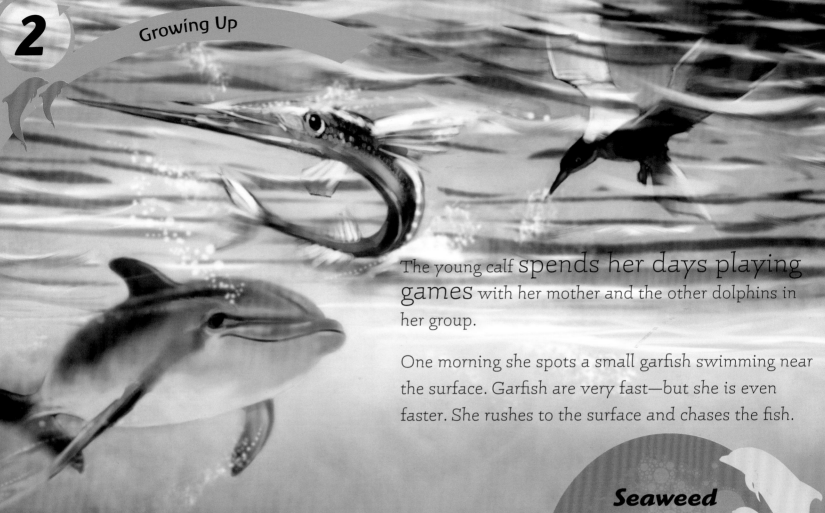

The young calf spends her days playing games with her mother and the other dolphins in her group.

One morning she spots a small garfish swimming near the surface. Garfish are very fast—but she is even faster. She rushes to the surface and chases the fish.

Just as she opens her mouth to grab the fish, a tern dives in and steals her meal! The young calf will have to be content to suckle milk from her mother for now.

Seaweed Games

Young dolphins often play games together with pieces of seaweed. This playtime helps teach the young dolphins how to chase and grab fish to eat.

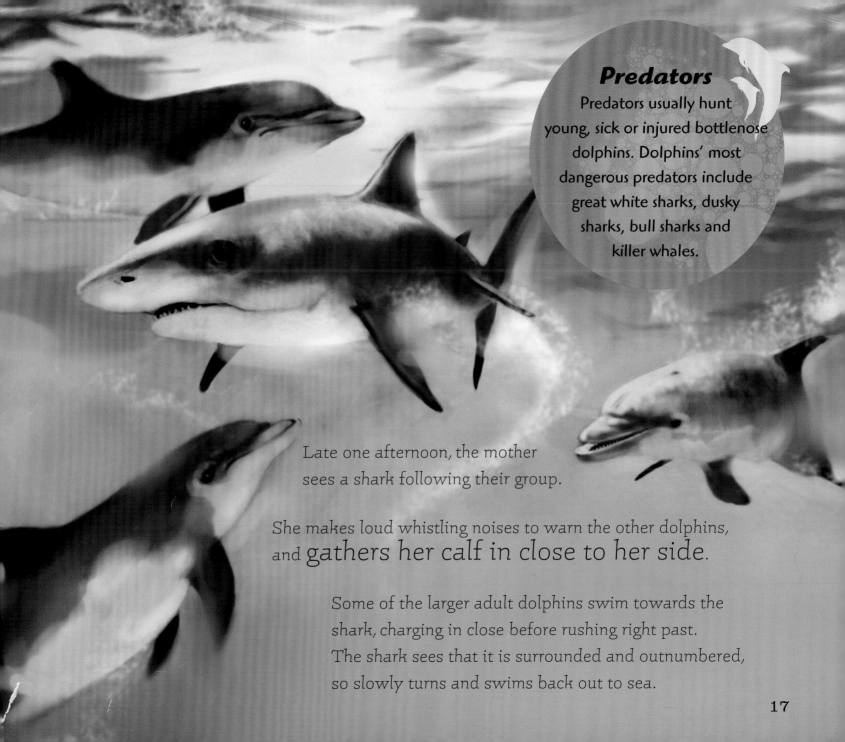

Predators

Predators usually hunt young, sick or injured bottlenose dolphins. Dolphins' most dangerous predators include great white sharks, dusky sharks, bull sharks and killer whales.

Late one afternoon, the mother sees a shark following their group.

She makes loud whistling noises to warn the other dolphins, and gathers her calf in close to her side.

Some of the larger adult dolphins swim towards the shark, charging in close before rushing right past. The shark sees that it is surrounded and outnumbered, so slowly turns and swims back out to sea.

17

The calf is growing and learning. It is now time for her to join the group on a hunt. The dolphins make loud clicking noises and listen for the clicks to bounce back off a school of fish.

An adult dolphin finds the school and organizes the other dolphins to surround it. They guide the fish toward shallow water then the dolphins take turns rushing through the school, grabbing the fish.

It is the calf's turn to grab a fish. She swims toward the panicked school as fast as she can. She misses the first fish, but grabs the second fish by the tail.

She shakes the fish to make sure it cannot escape and turns it around in her mouth. She swallows the fish head first.

Head First

Dolphins swallow fish head first. This stops the fish's spiky fins from getting stuck in the dolphin's throat.

She has proven herself as a predator and a useful member of the group. The more food she catches on her own, the less she needs to feed from her mother.

The young dolphin has grown into an adult. She is **catching her own food** and no longer needs t feed from her mother. She **stays with the group** as they continue to hunt together.

Early in the morning, the fish are slow and the water is still dark. Hunting in the morning gives the dolphins a better chance of catching a meal.

As the sun rises, the hunt turns to play as the dolphins **surf the waves** along their favourite beach.

Riding just beneath the surface, the young dolphin races along with the waves before **leaping** high out of the water.

Catching a Ride

Dolphins can get a free ride by surfing the waves created by large whales.

She spends most of the day playing in the waves. This helps her to **get to know the other dolphins** in her group.

Years have passed and now the dolphin **leads the group** as they chase down a large school of pilchards. However, a school of tuna has already moved in, eating as many fish as they can swallow. Hundreds of gannets have also joined this **feeding frenzy**.

The dolphins also feed on the fish. Before long, every last pilchard has been eaten.

Once a small, helpless calf, the dolphin has now grown into a large, strong and healthy female. She has learned many ways to find and hunt for food. She can even use sound to find fish that are hiding under the sand!

Now that she can take care of herself, it is time for her to mate and have a calf of her own.

23

One morning, as the group is swimming along the beach, they are joined by two male bottlenose dolphins. The males sense that the female is **ready to have a calf**, so they each mate with her.

After the males have mated with her several times, they leave. Soon she becomes **pregnant** and a calf begins to grow inside her. She is eating for two now, so she must eat whenever she can.

Twelve months after she became pregnant,
her belly has become very swollen. It is
time for her to give birth.

She swims into the warm water close to
the shore and gives birth to a calf. She
gently nudges the calf, helping it to the
surface, where it can take its first breath.

She has completed her life cycle. Now she
must help her calf grow and continue the cycle of life.

Threats to the Survival of Bottlenose Dolphins

Throughout their life cycle, bottlenose dolphins face many threats to their survival. Some of these threats come from natural events, while others come from people.

Natural Threats

From the moment a dolphin is born, it faces many dangers. Large predators feed on young, sick and injured dolphins.

Sharks

Large sharks, such as great white sharks and tiger sharks, feed on dolphins. They mostly hunt young or weak dolphins. Healthy, full-grown dolphins are usually fast enough to escape any shark that tries to eat them.

Killer Whales

Although an attack has never been observed, it is believed that killer whales occasionally hunt bottlenose dolphins.

Threats From Disease

Diseases can cause dolphins to become very sick or even die. Injuries can also become infected, which can cause dolphins to become very sick. Sick dolphins are easier to catch and are often killed by predators.

Great white sharks feed on sick and injured dolphins.

Human Threats

The biggest threat to the survival of dolphins comes from people. Humans contribute to the death of thousands of dolphins every year. People can harm dolphins in many different ways. Human activities have an effect on dolphin habitats and food, and on the dolphins themselves.

Fishing

Fishing kills thousands of dolphins every year. Dolphins can be killed accidentally when they become tangled in fishing nets. Driftnets more than 30 miles (50 kilometers) long float in the ocean, catching anything that swims past. When dolphins become tangled in the nets, they cannot swim. When they cannot swim to the surface to breathe, they drown.

Dolphin for Dinner?

In some countries, such as Japan, dolphins are hunted for food. There are many people who try to stop the killing and eating of dolphins and whales.

Driftnets kill hundreds of dolphins every year.

Pollution

Pollution can harm dolphins in many different ways. Dolphins may become tangled in garbage, such as old fishing lines. As dolphins grow, the fishing lines can cut into their skin, causing nasty injuries.

Chemicals that are dumped in the ocean can also harm dolphins. This type of pollution can cause diseases in dolphins and make them very sick. It can also damage their habitat, leaving the dolphins with nowhere to live and no food to eat.

Noise Pollution

Dolphins rely on sound to hunt and communicate. Noise from boats and construction can interfere with a dolphin's ability to find and catch food. This can force dolphins to move away from an area.

Pollution on beaches can be washed into the ocean, where it can harm marine animals such as bottlenose dolphins.

Habitat Destruction

When people build houses and factories near the water, they may damage coastal habitats. When these coastal habitats are destroyed, smaller **marine** animals can no longer find food or shelter. If there are no smaller animals, dolphins will have nothing to eat.

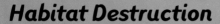

Dolphins in Captivity

Dolphins living in **captivity** do not live as long as dolphins in the wild. Many dolphins die from stress or disease soon after being captured.

If dolphin habitats are destroyed by building work and industry, dolphins will not be able to survive.

How Can You Help Protect Bottlenose Dolphins?

To protect any animal, we must protect its habitat. As well as not harming dolphins, people must protect the oceans where dolphins live and breed. Only then will they be able to survive and continue their life cycles.

Protect Our Oceans

Protecting our oceans is important for all creatures on Earth, including humans. People get a lot of their food from the ocean. If we destroy and pollute it, people and animals will not survive. You can help protect our oceans from pollution by putting your rubbish in a bin. This will keep it from blowing into the ocean, where it can cause so much harm.

Dolphins are beautiful to watch in the wild—from a distance. If you see a dolphin, do not feed it or it will depend on humans and not be able to look after itself

Join a Group

Many organizations have been set up to try and protect dolphins and other marine creatures. If more people support these groups, there is a better chance that these animals and our oceans can be saved.

Tell a Friend!

Share your love of dolphins with someone else and show them how special dolphins are. The more that people know and care about dolphins, the more they will want to help.

Glossary

adapted	changed to suit a particular way of living
blubber	fat under the skin
breed	produce young
captivity	held in zoos or parks
carnivores	animals that eat meat
estuaries	places where a river meets the sea
evolved	changed over time
extinct	no longer alive on the planet
habitat	the place where an animal, plant or other living thing lives
marine	related to the oceans or seas
mate	when a male and female come together to produce young
pollution	waste that harms the environment
predator	animal that eats other animals
pregnant	have young growing inside
prey	animals that are eaten by other animals
reproduce	have young
species	groups of animals or plants with similar features

Index